Original title:
Forget-Me-Not Fables

Copyright © 2025 Creative Arts Management OÜ
All rights reserved.

Author: Olivia Sterling
ISBN HARDBACK: 978-1-80566-699-8
ISBN PAPERBACK: 978-1-80566-984-5

Legends of Lost Petals

In a garden where petals danced bright,
A snail claimed he could take flight.
He strapped on a leaf, oh what a sight,
The wind blew hard, it gave him a fright.

The flowers giggled, they shook with glee,
As the snail tumbled down from a tree.
"Next time," he said, "I'll skip the tea,
And maybe just stick to my leafy spree!"

Remnants of the Wistful Blooms

Once a bloom with a quirky face,
Wished to win a bloom-fairy race.
With petals tied in a hasty lace,
She tripped on dew, fell flat on her grace.

The fairies laughed, spun round in glee,
"You're just a clumsy little pea!"
But she smiled wide, pointed with glee,
"I may trip, but I still can see!"

Chronicles of the Hidden Garden

In a garden so secret, so very confined,
Lived a bee who thought he was refined.
He buzzed in circles, terribly blind,
Until he realized he wasn't quite aligned.

With a hiccup and whirl, he changed his tune,
And danced with a bloom under the moon.
The garden chuckled, played a monsoon,
As the bee brought chaos with a silly cartoon!

Echoes of Blue in the Wind

There once was a blue flower, proud and spry,
Claimed he could reach up and touch the sky.
He waited for clouds, all fluffy and high,
But the wind just laughed, 'You still gotta try!'

With a gusty whoosh, he twisted around,
His laughter erupted, a joyous sound.
"I may not fly, but I'm garden-bound,
With friends like these, true joy is found!"

The Tapestry of Blooming Memories

In a garden where giggles grow,
Petals gossip, and daisies know.
Bees wear hats, oh what a sight,
While sunflowers dance under the light.

A buttercup plays hide and seek,
With clouds that chuckle, soft and meek.
Snapdragons snort with each little breeze,
While violets share their cheesy teas.

Fables Beneath the Canopy of Stars

Under the stars, stories weave,
A squirrel dons a suit, quite naive.
Owls hoot puns in their velvet night,
While fireflies twinkle, oh what a sight!

Once a rabbit wore shoes too big,
He tripped on a tale and danced a jig.
Mice in jackets, they swing and sway,
Telling tall tales until break of day.

Petal Secrets of Olden Days

Petals whisper secrets of yore,
With tales of antics and much, much more.
Rosebud's tales about a runny nose,
And how the dandelion lost her clothes.

In the shade of a lilac's giggle,
A snail told a tale that made us wiggle.
Old tulips recounted their prom nights,
How they danced till dawn, oh the delights!

The Fade of Unforgotten Tales

In the air, there's laughter that fades,
Like a picnic missed in leafy glades.
A wise old tree sighs tales of his youth,
While the sparrows squawk hilarious truth.

When laughter lingers like morning dew,
And clovers giggle, sharing a view.
Forgetful ants march in a line,
Recalling yesterday's cheese – so divine!

Beacons of Elusive Joy

In the garden of giggles, we play,
Chasing shadows that dance in the day.
A squirrel in glasses reads a book,
Pondering life while we steal a look.

Laughter erupts like bubbles in air,
Tickling noses, a comical flare.
The daisies chuckle, the roses tease,
In this realm of whimsy, we aim to please.

Chronicles in the Breeze

Whispers of mischief float on the wind,
A kite steals a cookie, a daring sin.
While daisies plot the next great caper,
A bee dons a hat, a buzzing draper.

Clouds giggle softly, dressed in white fluff,
While the sun throws confetti, saying, 'That's enough!'
Each breeze tells tales of truly strange sights,
As laughter pirouettes on the back of light.

The Whimsical Veil of Time

Time wears a tutu, twirls with delight,
As minutes skip rope under the moonlight.
An hourglass winks with a sparkle and grin,
While seconds throw parties, let the fun begin.

Old clocks are jealous of the sounds we make,
As laughter fills spaces, never a mistake.
Giggles and chuckles, a cheerful parade,
In the land of the silly, memories are made.

Hidden in the Beauty of Blooms

Petals wear hats, they're dressed to impress,
Bumblebees gossip, creating a mess.
A tulip's joke leaves everyone gasping,
While pansies host parties, brightly clasping.

In the meadow's embrace, the mischief grows,
A daffodil dances, striking silly poses.
Amidst nature's humor, we find our delight,
As flowers tickle our hearts, oh what a sight!

Reveries of Tender Times

Once a flower wore a hat,
Said it's quite the latest chat!
A bumblebee gave it a glance,
Then swayed to an awkward dance.

The petals whispered silly things,
About the joy that springtime brings.
A squirrel giggled from the tree,
'You've got more style than me!'

With sunshine, laughter filled the air,
Wooing all those who'd stop and stare.
While daisies cracked a cheeky grin,
These memories, where to begin?

As twilight approached with a snicker,
The flowers held hands, growing thicker.
"I'll take your jokes, if you take mine!"
They promised a friendship divine.

The Language of Forgotten Flowers

In a garden, blooms would chat,
One wore glasses, quite the brat!
Telling tales of garden gnomes,
Who stole the seeds, and lived like foam.

But interlaced within their prattle,
A rose declared, 'Let's have a battle!'
'You think your jokes are very slick,
I'll out-pun you, just watch this trick!'

Together, they laughed at the sun,
As bees flew by, darted for fun.
'These tales shall grow, just give a shout,
We'll pickle laughter, toss it about!'

So in whispers, secrets got spun,
From petals young to roots undone.
A tulip snickered, 'Is that a jest?
Or just pollen stuck to its chest?'

Silent Witnesses of Time

In lands where whispers walk with ease,
Flowers giggle in the breeze.
They've seen long stories, love and tears,
And yet they sprout with no more fears.

A daffodil said, 'Did you see,
The sun trip over that old tree?'
While violets blushed with pure delight,
'Gotta love the drama of the night!'

As bumblebees buzzed in a fleet,
The lilies joked, 'This pollination's neat!'
Time might pass, but friendship's bright,
Turning dull days to sheer delight.

So join the laughter, it's not a chore,
These blooms are legends, always wanting more.
In laughter, we find our lasting traces,
Silent witnesses to light-filled places.

Lyrics of Vanishing Light

When shadows stretch and daylight flops,
The daisies plot with cheery hops.
They sing of moonlight's funny face,
And dance around, a having grace.

A marigold flaunts its golden crown,
'Who's the fairest in this town?'
The roses chime, 'We're all quite nice,
But don't forget, we've got our spice!'

With giggles glittering in the dusk,
The flowers share secrets, free from musk.
Each petal tells a joke or two,
And blooms beneath the twilight hue.

So gather 'round as colors blend,
A botanical bash where smiles extend.
In the realm of evening light,
We write our songs with pure delight.

The tapestry of Blooming Hearts

In a garden full of chatter,
The daisies spilled some tea,
A butterfly, a curious matter,
Tried to join in glee.

The tulips wore their brightest hats,
While roses danced a jig,
A cabbage laughed at all the chitchats,
Said, "Oh, you folks are big!"

A bumblebee, in search of fun,
Flew in circles, lost the plot,
Under the sun, all joy begun,
Silly flowers in a knot.

When evening falls, they share the tales,
Of mischief and of dreams,
In the breeze, the laughter sails,
Blooming hearts and silly schemes.

Stories That Dance on the Breeze

Once a snail with a grand old tale,
Claimed he'd run a race,
The rabbit laughed and said, "Not a chance,"
"You'll never pick up pace!"

The crowd cheered on from the side,
A tortoise stole a wink,
But just as hope began to slide,
The snail started to think.

With every inch, he told his plot,
Of mountains high and wide,
And the rabbit paused, his laughter caught,
Could this slow one turn the tide?

So stories danced like leaves in spring,
On breezes full of jest,
A race of thoughts, the laughter's ring,
Turns slow to quick, the best.

Echoes of Laughter in the Fields

In fields where grass tickles toes,
A scarecrow cracked a joke,
The crows rolled over, struck a pose,
Said, "This will make us choke!"

The daisies chimed with giggles sweet,
As rabbits hopped in time,
Each ripple in the grass was neat,
Creating a playful rhyme.

Even ants joined in this fun,
With tiny little cheers,
A party under the blazing sun,
Where laughter chased away fears.

Echoes bounced 'tween tree and stone,
In fields of pure delight,
Together, never felt alone,
They danced through day and night.

Shimmering in the Twilight

As stars began to peek and shine,
A fox put on a show,
With juggling fireflies, oh so fine,
The audience went 'whoa!'

A raccoon clapped his clever paws,
At every twist and turn,
He said, "Now folks, let's give applause,
For this is how we learn!"

The moon smiled wide upon the scene,
With laughter warm and bright,
Illuminating all that's keen,
In the shimmering twilight.

And as the world embraced the night,
The critters danced away,
With echoes of their pure delight,
In twilight's sweet ballet.

Stories Woven in Nature's Hand

In a field where daisies tease,
A rabbit danced with utmost ease.
He wore a hat, oh so grand,
While juggling carrots, quite unplanned.

A butterfly, with grace obscene,
Taught the squirrel to act quite mean.
They played pranks 'neath the old oak,
Until the tree began to choke.

A wise old turtle told them true,
"Nature's fun, but don't overdo!"
Yet off they went, in joyful spree,
Finding trouble, glee, and glee.

So if you see them laugh and play,
In fields where sunlight warms the day,
Just join the game, forget your fate,
In nature's tales, just celebrate!

Enigmas of the Sapphire Flower

Amongst the petals, bright and blue,
A bee danced in the morning dew.
He wore a tie, quite out of place,
Buzzing jokes with a funny face.

A wise old fox with spectacles,
Declared the mysteries of the bells.
"What's in a name? I cannot tell!"
But laughed so loud, he broke the spell.

With whispers shared through swirling leaves,
The flowers giggled like cheeky thieves.
Hidden secrets, hidden quest,
In this bloom, you'd find the best!

So wander forth with laughter bright,
Chase the mysteries with delight.
For who knows what may take flight,
In flowers where the fairy lights!

The Dance of Faded Elegance

Once a rose with a limp so grand,
Put on a show, thought it'd be planned.
With wobbly steps and a spin so wide,
It fell and giggled, twirled with pride.

Nearby a tulip laughed out loud,
"Oh dear rose, you're way too proud!"
Together they frolicked under the moon,
Leaving crickets to hum a tune.

The lilacs joined with a sway and twist,
Creating a dance that none could resist.
With petals flying and roots that twirled,
In a whimsical world, colors swirled.

So if you see the flowers sway,
Join this dance without delay!
For in their laughs, life seems to blend,
In faded elegance that will not end!

Lullabies Amidst the Blossoming Silence

In the meadow, soft and sweet,
A cricket sang to the beetles fleet.
"Hush now, dear bugs, no need to fight,
Let's sing our lullabies tonight!"

A sleepy snail with dreams of cheese,
Swayed along in the gentle breeze.
With rhythmic hums that rose and fell,
In nature's choir, all was swell.

The daisies closed their eyes so tight,
While fireflies sparkled with golden light.
As stars peeked down, the night grew bold,
The lullabies of flowers, stories told.

So come, my friend, let's softly lay,
Under blossoms and stars, we'll stay.
For in this silence, whispers roam,
Nature's heart, our cozy home.

Labyrinth of Blue Memories

In a maze of hues so bright,
Lived a squirrel that took to flight.
He forgot his acorn stash,
And now it's all a flash!

With a hat too big to wear,
He danced without a care.
Birds chirped a silly tune,
While he pranced around at noon.

Chasing shadows, sipping dreams,
He chased butterflies and screams.
But when he tripped on his toe,
He laughed, 'What a funny show!'

In this twist of furry fate,
He learned to enjoy the gait.
Each stumble just a jest,
Living life to the fullest jest!

Gardens Intertwined

In a garden full of jest,
Roses whispered, 'We're the best!'
Tulips giggled, 'What a bluff!'
While daisies said, 'Oh, enough!'

A bumblebee flew in a haste,
Wound up late for the sweet taste.
He buzzed around in a whirl,
Yelling, 'Boy, what a twirl!'

Sunflowers leaned to share a joke,
And even thorns had a poke.
Laughter bloomed in every nook,
Nature's park, a funny book!

When the raindrops joined the fun,
They fell like giggles, one by one.
In this garden filled with cheer,
Every petal held a dear!

Notes from the Silent Bloom

A flower wrote a little note,
To a bee, smart and remote.
'If you buzz my name in rhyme,
I'll offer nectar every time!'

But the bee flew past too fast,
Said he'd come, but forgot at last.
Now the flower, proud and bright,
Chortled, 'What a funny sight!'

With petals waving in the breeze,
It tickled leaves and teased trees.
Holding secrets of the night,
They giggled, 'What a funny plight!'

Underneath the moon so grand,
They whispered jokes across the land.
Every bloom had tales to weave,
In laughter's web, we do believe!

Titles Untold in Nature's Embrace

In a forest deep and wide,
A bear tried to dance with pride.
He slipped and rolled in leaves so green,
What a sight, a funny scene!

A rabbit watched with a grin,
Chuckling at the bear's spin.
'You call that a dance move, friend?'
The bear just laughed, 'I'll pretend!'

Meanwhile, an owl hooted wise,
Wearing a cap with bright blue eyes.
'You're a dancer, not a fool!'
As the forest laughed, oh, what a jewel!

When the dusk gave way to night,
Creatures rejoiced in pure delight.
With stories whispered through the leaves,
In nature's arms, humor weaves!

Whispers of the Blue Petals

A flower spoke to a bumblebee,
"Do I look like a fancy TV?"
The bee just laughed, buzzing with glee,
"You're a beauty, but don't make me flee!"

In the garden, the daisies danced,
While a silly snail looked quite entranced.
"A race! A race!" he boldly pranced,
But ended up snoozing, quite unenhanced!

A gossiping spider spun a tall tale,
Of how she rode on a giant's tail.
Her friends just chuckled, "Oh, do not bail!
You're more knotted up than a fish with a scale!"

And as the sun dipped down once more,
The petals giggled, wishing for more.
In this garden where laughter did soar,
Every bloom held a secret to explore.

A Tale of Fleeting Memories

Once a daffodil wore a bright crown,
Claiming the title of best in town.
But the wind took his hat, and he frowned,
"I wanted to be the toast, not down!"

In the patch, a rabbit hopped by,
With radishes stuck in his eye.
"What's happening?" asked a curious fly,
"I thought you'd be faster than a pie!"

A busy old tortoise sighs, "Oh dear,
I always forget where I put my gear!"
But a nearby snail said, "Don't you fear,
Forgetting's just fun, like drinking some beer!"

So in this garden of memory's play,
Each silly blossom has something to say.
With laughter and joy, they twist and sway,
Creating tales that brighten the day.

The Bloom of Remembrance

A rose was prancing with glittering flair,
Declared, "I'm the fairest, just look at my hair!"
But a petunia said, "You're quite the chare,
That wind's got your style in quite a snare!"

A bumblebee named Max flew with sass,
Said, "I remember you worked with class!
But if we're wearing sequins, you've got to pass—
You look more like a glammed-up grass!"

In the soil, earthworms quietly gossiped,
"Did you hear what the tulips just whispered?"
Then they erupted with laughter, not stopped,
"Was that glamour or just over-nipped?"

In this garden of blooms, bold and bright,
Every petal giggles in pure delight.
With tales of the silly under moonlight,
They conjure up joy from morning till night.

Echoes of the Past Garden

Amidst the flowers, an old garden creeps,
The daisies chuckle as the onion weeps.
"Why so sad?" the sunflower peeps,
"Did you forget, or just take long leaps?"

A quirky crow cawed, "You should all know,
I flew past the moon, put on quite a show!
But honestly, I couldn't tell you though,
If I saw a bright star or a big yellow glow!"

A mischievous cat snuck by with a grin,
Claimed, "I'm here to gather tales from within!"
But he tripped over daisies with a spin,
And tumbled, declaring, "Let the fun begin!"

As the shadows stretch and the sun turns low,
These colorful sights put on quite the show.
With memories playful, they're sure to grow,
In this garden of laughter, where mischief flows.

Tales from a Blue Horizon

In a land where daisies giggle,
Laughter tickles every little wiggle.
A turtle lost his shell in a race,
Now he wears a fruit bowl on his face.

A cat with shoes danced on the lawn,
While chickens sang a silly song.
They all gathered for a tea party fair,
With cupcakes flying through the air!

A squirrel tried to play the drum,
But the beat went, 'Thump and thud and bumm.'
The ant brigade joined in with glee,
Marching to the tune of 'Ode to Me.'

So let the tales of laughter unfold,
In bizarre antics and bright tales told.
For in the blue horizon's sight,
Laughter springs like morning light.

Secrets Written in the Breeze.

A whisper floats upon the wind,
Of a goose who wished to play the violin.
He feathered his bow with a fishy tale,
Plucking strings made the whole pond wail!

A rabbit wore socks, mismatched and bright,
Claiming it's fashion, not a silly sight.
With each hop, he twirled in glee,
Chasing shadows of the dancing bee.

The clouds above took notes on a whim,
As a fly performed a solo grim.
Yet the sun burst out with a grin so wide,
Turning blunders into a joyful ride!

Secrets carried by the playful breeze,
Dancing with glee among the trees.
In nature's humor and laughter rife,
Every silly moment adds to life.

Whispers of the Silent Bloom

In a garden where the flowers tell,
A cactus tried to run, oh well!
He tripped on petals, flew with a shout,
Bouncing back in giggles throughout.

The roses held a secret debate,
Claiming their thorns were just first-rate.
But violets chimed in, 'We smell so sweet!
No need for sharp points, we don't compete!'

A dandelion puff would drift and sway,
Booking his flight on a windy day.
With a twist and a twirl, he'd lightly zoom,
Telling the sun about his blooming doom.

So hush your ears, for tales are weaved,
Of blossoms bright and leaves believed.
In whispers soft, they spin the yarn,
Of the silly world where laughter's born.

Legends Under the Blue Petal

Beneath the blue petal, a story unfolds,
Of a snail who fancied riches and gold.
He donned a hat made of sparkling dew,
Chasing dreams that fluttered and flew.

A bug with a trumpet played jazz in the night,
While fireflies twinkled, oh what a sight!
A worm joined in, jamming with flair,
Claiming he'd dance if he had some air.

The moon peeked down with a twinkle and grin,
As a mischievous frog jumped in to win.
With a splash and a leap, he stole the show,
Making the daisies sway to and fro.

Under the blue petal, legends are spun,
Of humorous mishaps and laughter begun.
For in this haven, where giggles flow,
Every creature's episode steals the show!

A Garden of Silent Voices

In a garden where whispers play,
Plants gossip about the day.
The sunflower tried to tell a joke,
But the daisies just sat there, broke.

Rabbits hop with secret glee,
Wishing for a cup of tea.
While bees buzz out silly tunes,
Underneath the laughing moons.

The carrots sneak a dance or two,
But the spinach just won't come through.
A head of lettuce hugs a tree,
Shouting, 'Why won't you dance with me?'

So in this garden, laughter blooms,
Among the silent, leafy rooms.
With voices low and giggles high,
Even flowers might just fly.

Fragments of What Was

Memories float like leaves in air,
Dancing high without a care.
A wilted rose recalls a date,
But the thorns just sneer at fate.

The echo of a fabled tale,
Where socks went missing, small and pale.
They ventured off to find a mate,
Now they lounge on a sunny plate.

Once a garden, now a plot,
Where daffodils forgot their spot.
They're mingling with the weeds, it's true,
But both agree, 'We're quite a crew!'

So take this tale with humor bright,
For even lost socks find the light.
And fragments of a past long gone,
Can still make us chuckle on.

Threads of Nostalgia

Threads of memory weave and twist,
In a patch where joy can't be missed.
Button eyes on the fabric loom,
Wink at shadows, chase away gloom.

Knitting tales of the days gone by,
Where the skies were blue, oh my!
A scarf remembers every hug,
While the yarn dances, snug as a bug.

Each stitch a wink from time once lost,
A tapestry of laughter tossed.
So let's unravel each old seam,
And knit anew, a brand-new dream.

In the fabric of our lives we find,
Nostalgia's threads that rewind.
So laugh and sew with heart so free,
For each memory's a jubilee.

Blooming in the Shadows

In corners where the light won't peek,
Funny flowers start to speak.
With petals tucked like shy romance,
They giggle softly, take a chance.

A daffodil, a bit absurd,
Told a joke that went unheard.
'Why did the gardener carry a spade?'
'Because the lawn had misbehaved!'

Mushrooms pop up, sprightly, bold,
With secrets of the earth retold.
They wink at rocks, they spin and twirl,
In stillness, chaos starts to whirl.

So bloom where shadows dare to play,
In laughter's arms, we find a way.
With giggles light and colors bright,
Let's dance in shadows, pure delight.

Wishing Wells and Petal Dreams

In a well where dreams take flight,
A fish with shoes danced in the night.
He twirled and spun with such delight,
Chasing stars with all his might.

A cat in boots sang silly songs,
While frogs played chess with little gongs.
Each laugh echoed, where joy belongs,
In the land where nothing's wrong.

Butterflies tell the silliest tales,
Of traveling trains and windy gales.
A snail once tried to ride on rails,
But fell asleep; oh, how it fails!

Wishing wells bring such odd charm,
With jellybeans as sweet as farm.
With every joke, who needs alarm?
In this world, we're safe from harm.

Sketches of Lost Moments

A squirrel with a monocle sits wise,
Drawing maps of berry pies.
He runs a shop, a cute disguise,
For customers who want some fries.

A turtle lost his marbles once,
A crowd of mice began to dance.
They spun around, oh what a bunch,
Until they fell—what a great chance!

A cloud with polka dots rolls by,
While kittens try to touch the sky.
They leap and flip, oh my, oh my!
But land in puddles, oh how they cry!

Sketches made with giggles and cheers,
Filled with crayons and silly gears.
Lost moments turn to burst of tears,
But laughter follows through the years.

Shadows of a Gentle Breeze

A shadow danced beneath the trees,
Wiggling toes in a playful tease.
It whispered secrets with such ease,
And tickled noses with the breeze.

Birds in hats flew by with flair,
Spreading gossip—what a pair!
They squawked about a missing chair,
And laughed at dreams alive in air.

The sun rolled down to join the fun,
Chasing shadows until they run.
It painted smiles, every one,
And played hide-and-seek till done.

In this land where laughter thrives,
Where every giggle surely dives.
We find the joy, the silly drives,
Amidst the breeze where laughter jives.

Gardens of the Wild Heart

In gardens where the wild hearts bloom,
A raccoon wears a polka-dot costume.
He juggles fruits, avoiding doom,
While birds cheer loudly in the room.

The flowers gossip with the bees,
About a snail who likes to tease.
He thinks he's fast, oh what a tease,
But trips on grass, it's sure to please!

A butterfly painted like a pie,
Claims to be too fancy to fly.
Yet, when it tries to catch the sky,
It flutters low with a funny sigh.

Gardens bloom with smiles and cheer,
Each petal flipping through the year.
In wild hearts, there's nothing to fear,
Just laughter ringing ever near.

Echoes Between Yesterday and Tomorrow

When squirrels gossip under the tree,
They whisper tales too tall for me.
A sandwich lost, it travels far,
In dreams it rides a tiny car.

The books we read, they laugh out loud,
About a cow that danced with a crowd.
Yet, in the end, they all agree,
Tomorrow's lunch is lost to me.

Our socks play hide and seek all night,
One's a hero, the other's slight.
They claim together they can fly,
But really, they're just pie in the sky.

So here's to days of fun and jest,
When nonsense rules, and we can rest.
In echoes past, we'll find our cheer,
And giggle at our yesteryear.

When Hearts Remember

Old dogs bark at clouds up high,
Claiming they're all birds that fly.
With every woof, they tell the tale,
Of chasing dreams on a fluffy sail.

The cats, they sit with knowing grins,
Plotting their reigns and future wins.
Yet fondly, they recall that time,
When they mistook wet paint for clime.

A child may giggle at a shoe,
Worn by a giant, perhaps it's true.
In slumber dreams, they're queens and kings,
A kingdom built with random things.

Hearts remember when we were small,
With secret wishes to embrace it all.
So let's dance with echoes, frolic bright,
In silly joy that takes to flight.

Secrets Beneath the Soil

The garden gnomes hold tales untold,
Of buried treasure made of gold.
Yet when we dig, we find it's beans,
A feast of soil, our silly dreams.

Worms in jackets plot their schemes,
To make the best of moonlit beams.
With every wiggle, they declare,
The earth is full of tasty fare.

In pots of mud, we plant our hopes,
And water them with silly ropes.
Each flower sings, but none can rhyme,
They all just dance with silly thyme.

So gather round the leafy green,
Where secrets sprout that can't be seen.
In laughter shared, the soil's deep,
Awakens thoughts to dream and leap.

The Stories We Leave Behind

In dusty books where laughter grows,
There lurk the heroes—tall tales and prose.
A sock that traveled 'neath the bed,
Claims it was once a lion, well-fed.

Our shoes have stories; how they roam,
From cobbled streets to unknown home.
Yet, in the closet, they conspire,
To weave a tale of wild desire.

The mischief of cats, the sighs of chairs,
They tell of ghosts with fluffy cares.
In every creak, a charming jest,
The stories linger, never rest.

So as we walk through lanes of time,
With laughter echoed in each rhyme,
Let's share the tales we find anew,
For every laugh, a love is true.

The Garden That Remembers

In the garden where daisies bloom,
A gnome lost his hat and found a broom.
The rabbits laugh as they hop around,
While the flowers giggle without a sound.

A squirrel tried to juggle seeds,
But slipped and fell among the weeds.
The roses snickered, 'Oh dear me!'
As the gnome now dances with glee.

The bees are buzzing a funny tune,
As daisies sway beneath the moon.
A picnic planned turns into a feast,
With ants that march, not afraid in the least.

In this garden, memories play,
While laughter sprinkles the sunlit day.
Every flower holds a story tight,
Making the weirdest moments just right.

Whispers from the Forgotten Hill

On a hill where shadows prance,
A ghost tells jokes, not a single chance.
With a wink and a laugh, he waves his hand,
While the trees dance, isn't it grand?

The owls hoot with a comedic flair,
As rabbits listen, without a care.
Each whisper winds like a playful breeze,
Tickling the leaves in mischievous tease.

A potato rolled down with a frown,
While a cabbage tried to wear a crown.
They fell in laughter, what a sight!
Turns out, veggies have humor at night!

The forgotten hill hums with glee,
As creatures plot their next spree.
With tales that echo in moonlit spills,
The laughter lives on, on forgotten hills.

Journeys through Shaded Lane

In shaded lanes where whispers roam,
A hedgehog carries his book of poems.
With a quill and ink, he scribbles tight,
Writing secrets that spark the night.

A turtle trotted, slow as can be,
Said, "Hurry up, I want to see!"
But the hedgehog paused, quite bemused,
As a rabbit hopped by, slightly confused.

They stumbled upon a curious snail,
Who claimed he had sailed on a grand gale.
With giggles galore under leafy shade,
The journey became an escapade!

Laughter echoed down the lane,
As friends made fun of a passing train.
In tales of whimsy, how time flies,
With shaded journeys under sunny skies.

Sunlight on Lingering Thoughts

When sunlight peeked through lazy clouds,
A cat wore sunglasses, feeling proud.
She sipped her tea, said, "This is nice!"
With a wave to the dog who was rolling dice.

A parrot squawked some silly jokes,
While frogs in a choir sang riddling blokes.
Each bird had a tale, bold and grand,
In the warmth of the sun, they made their stand.

A cloud drifted by, feeling left out,
So it formed into shapes that made them shout!
From bunnies to boats, the laughter poured,
Creating memories none could afford.

As daylight waned, they packed their thoughts,
Leaving behind the joy that's sought.
With sunlight fading, oh what a sight,
Lingering moments turned into delight.

Secrets in the Garden's Embrace

In the garden where daisies pirouette,
A squirrel dressed as a pirate, you bet!
He claims to defend a treasure of nuts,
But it's really just acorns, oh what a rutz!

Ladybugs gossip, without a doubt,
About flowers who never come out.
'What's the story?' asks a dandy bee,
'Did the tulip break up with the pea?'

Chronicles of the Tiny Blue Star

A tiny blue star on a petal sits,
Wishing it knew how to do backflips.
It dreams of the night and moon's silver glow,
But gets dizzy when it tries to flow.

Butterflies drift, wearing tiny top hats,
Debating with ants over cheesiest chats.
'Who's fanciest of all in this bright field?'
'That one!' they shout, 'the daisy's revealed!'

Alchemy of Remembrance and Blossom

In a pot of stew with a whiff of thyme,
The herbs start to waltz, oh what a crime!
Parsley and basil, they take the stage,
Guess who's the judge? A wise, old sage.

A tulip spills tea to a row of bugs,
Laughing aloud at the gossip it chugs.
'Did you see that bee wearing stripes on his back?
Looks like a walking candy, what a snack!'

The Fables of Timeless Blossoms

Once a rose dressed in pearls, meant to impress,
Stood tall in the garden, just a bit of a mess.
It slipped on some dew and did a pirouette,
All the daisies giggled, place your bets!

An elder sunflower shared tales of its past,
Saying bees were too slow, supposed to be fast.
But the bees just buzzed, 'Now that's some old news,
We've got pollen to gather, no time for snooze!'

Diary of Tiny Blooms

In the garden, blooms convene,
Whispering tales so often unseen.
One flower told of a sprightly bee,
Who danced with a twig on a grand jubilee.

A tulip giggled with petals spread wide,
'Watch out for rain!' it joked with great pride.
But clouds misunderstood this colorful quest,
And drenched all the blooms—oh, what a jest!

Each stem now swayed with laughter anew,
As droplets sparkled like morning dew.
In this patch, where mirth took its flight,
Tiny blooms giggle 'til late in the night.

The Hidden Stories of Time

Behind each leaf, a tale's been spun,
Of a snail who thought he could run!
He lost the race, met a swift little hare,
Who found that slow wins—how strange, yet fair!

An old oak listened, its roots in a twist,
To happenstance laughs that none could resist.
It shook off its leaves, letting secrets unfurl,
While squirrels plotted their nutty world.

From each blossom's edge, secrets escape,
With giggles and wiggles, the tales take shape.
Time's not a monster, or so said the vine,
It's merely a partner in stories divine.

Legends in Lavender

In lavender fields, tales twist and twirl,
Where a dandelion once caused a whirl.
He boasted his fluff could float to the moon,
But ended up lost in a sweet afternoon.

A lazy bee buzzed, claiming to know,
Where far-off dreams like a river could flow.
"Just follow your heart," said the wise sunflower,
Who had danced with the wind for many an hour.

So off with a jig went the playful plume,
To seek out the starlight in lavender bloom.
And laughter erupted from each fragrant sprout,
For all of them knew what life was about.

The Heart's Gentle Archive

In the attic of hearts, laughter's a key,
Unlocking the smiles of you and me.
With memories wrapped in ribbons of light,
Each giggle recorded in dreams of the night.

A diary written with petals and ink,
Where wishes and whispers are closer than you think.
Frogs tell stories beneath the moonbeam,
While fireflies dance like memories stream.

So here's to the moments that make us all grin,
In the archive of hearts, let the fun begin!
For every chuckle and wink that we save,
Is a thread in the quilt our joy loves to weave.

Blue Petals Across the Years

Blue petals dance and sway,
In a garden, bright and gay.
They giggle with the breeze,
And tease the buzzing bees.

A raccoon steals a snack,
While the flowers laugh, don't lack.
A squirrel joins the fun,
Sipping dew, he's second to none.

They throw a party, wild and loud,
With crickets chirping, feeling proud.
The moon looks down, wide-eyed,
As petals bounce like they've been fried.

When morning comes, they play it cool,
Pretending they're the garden school.
But watch out for the hungry plight—
The gardener's dog, ready to bite!

The Dreamer's Garden

In a garden where dreams grow,
Bumblebees perform a show.
Tulips wear their fanciest hats,
While roses giggle at the chitchats.

A pizza slice falls from a tree,
The rabbits shout, "Oh, look at me!"
They munch and crunch with delight,
And dance until the fall of night.

The fairies sip on tea so sweet,
Trading secrets, quite the feat.
They poke fun at stoic signs,
Who guard the pot of glimmering vines.

And when the sun begins to set,
The garden whispers, "Don't regret!"
For if you dream and laugh aloud,
You'll join the quirkiest crowd.

Ephemeral Beauty

A flower blooms, then takes a bow,
It's beauty fades, don't ask me how.
The daisies giggle, "What a scene!
We're off to the ball, so serene!"

They twirl and swirl in a sunny glow,
Chasing shadows, putting on a show.
"Oh dear, where did the violets go?"
They faded fast; like magical snow.

The dandelions play peek-a-boo,
With wind, they wander—oh, what a view!
"Catch me if you can!" they tease the sun,
In this game of chaos, they sure have fun.

But time will paint with strokes so fine,
As petals drift like playful wine.
Embrace the giggles from blooms so bright,
For laughter holds the secret light.

The Heart's Quiet Revolt

The heart whispered, "I'm tired today,"
Underneath roses, in disarray.
"Let's wear our best, join in the spree,
For life's too short; let's dance, you'll see!"

With floppy hats and mismatched socks,
They prance around like silly clocks.
An owl hoots, "What's the fuss?
With all this joy, there's no need to rush!"

The daisies chuckle, causing a stir,
"Who needs a reason? Just taste the blur!"
While thorns compete for a tricky rhyme,
Tick-tock, tick-tock; it's party time!

So let the heart lead the fun parade,
With laughter and blooms, none will fade.
A peaceful revolt, a sweet little game,
Where joy reigns supreme, never the same.

Echoes Beneath the Flower's Veil

In a garden so lively and bright,
The daisies gossip, oh what a sight!
With tulips that giggle, they all conspire,
Plotting pranks that might take you higher.

A dandelion's wish took flight in the breeze,
"Catch me if you can!" to the curious bees.
But as the sun sets, they laugh and they sway,
Planning more antics for the next sunny day.

With petals for crowns, they hold silly court,
Where daisies wear dreams, and blooms hold a sport.
Bumbling bugs join in with a jig and a spin,
Who knew flowers could dance? Let the fun begin!

So come, wander this garden so rich,
Where laughter and blooms are our favorite niche.
Echoes of joy beneath scents all around,
These silly flower tales by nature are found.

Tales of the Fleeting Flora

Once in a meadow, the sun danced so bright,
Petals stretched out in a comical fight.
"Who's the prettiest?" shouted the rose,
While violets giggled, striking funny poses.

Bumble bees bounced with fabulous flair,
Chasing each other through fragrant air.
"Catch the pollen!" they buzzed with glee,
As daisies snickered at the bumblebee spree.

The lilacs came in with a grand pirouette,
While poppies cried out, "We're not done yet!"
With laughter and joy, the blossoms took flight,
In a comical race 'neath the moon's silver light.

In a world where the flowers know how to jest,
Life blooms with humor, and we are so blessed.
These fleeting moments we cherish so dear,
In the tales of the flora that tickle our cheer.

Memories Wrought in Petal Threads

Once a daffodil wore socks of bright green,
And danced in the breeze like a frolicking bean.
The others just chuckled, "What a cute sight!"
As the sun winked down with sheer delight.

A peony plotted a game in the shade,
While marigolds whispered of pranks they had made.
"Let's tie up the wind and make him our friend!"
Oh, the memories spun as the laughter won't end.

With blossoms so colorful, secrets they share,
Of funny mishaps and whimsical care.
They weave their own tales in the soft morning light,
Petal threads binding them, making life bright.

So join in the fun where the minutes take flight,
Amongst these wild wonders that sparkle the night.
In the laughter of flowers, let your heart sing,
For memories once made can be the sweetest thing.

The Language of Delicate Blooms

In the hush of the twilight, blooms start to chat,
The roses debate on who's the best hat.
"Look at my petals, they shimmer and shine!"
While violets giggle, "Now that's just divine!"

A sunflower stretched, with a grin oh so wide,
"Let's play hide-and-seek, just you and I!"
Petals whispered secrets, oh what a crew,
As daisies danced lightly, in the sweet morning dew.

In gardens where laughter takes root in the clay,
The blooms tell their tales in their own special way.
A language of giggles, and colors ablaze,
Creating a story in sunshine and haze.

So lend me your ear to these delicate sounds,
Where joy pops like bubbles and magic abounds.
In the world of the flowers, fun never ends,
In the symphony blooming, where laughter transcends.

Serenades of the Wistful Meadow

In a meadow of dreams, where daisies dance,
A rabbit named Timmy wore his best pants.
He sang to the flowers, oh what a delight,
But tripped on a snail, oh what a sight!

The sun did play tricks, casting shadows so sly,
While butterflies giggled, oh my, oh my!
Timmy just laughed, he dusted his nose,
And twirled with the daisies, in their bright clothes.

The ants all applauded, a silly parade,
As Timmy performed a wiggly charade.
With giggles and wiggles, they stole the show,
In a meadow of joy, where all love to go.

So here's to the fables of laughter and cheer,
In a land where the flowers are all full of beer.
For each little mishap gives reason to grin,
In the meadow of dreams, let the laughter begin!

Shadows in the Blue Meadow

In a meadow so blue, lived a cheeky old goat,
He thought he could dance, and he thought he could float.
He leaped on a log, in the soft summer grass,
Fell right on his back, what a comical class!

The shadows all clustered, with giggles and grins,
As they watched the goat struggle to show them his spins.
He jumped once again, with a twirl and a flap,
But landed in mud, oh, what a mishap!

A wise old bluebird chirped, with a knowing glance,
"Oh, silly old goat, stop trying to prance!"
But he just rolled over, with laughter so bright,
In the shadows they danced, what a whimsical sight!

So if you should wander to that meadow so blue,
Remember the goat and his muddy debut.
For shadows remind us, through all of our falls,
Life's a dance, my friends, and laughter enthralls!

Songs of the Heart's Remembrance

Underneath the sunshine, where the daisies grow,
A bumblebee named Buzz sang a soft hello.
He tried to play music on a flower's horn,
But the petal just giggled, 'Oh dear, I'm torn!'

With tunes that were silly, Buzz flew with flair,
But got stuck in a thistle, oh what a scare!
His friends all surrounded, with chuckles so wide,
As he wiggled and jiggled, they couldn't hide.

Then came a wise ladybug, spotted and grand,
"Buzz, dear, you must learn to play in a band!"
He nodded and promised to sing just the right,
While they all joined the chorus, what a joyful sight!

So gather the blooms, and the critters who hum,
In the meadow of laughter, let the joy come.
For each little melody dances with cheer,
In songs of the heart, let the smiles appear!

The Myth of the Gentle Petal

Once in a garden, there bloomed a fine rose,
Who claimed that her fragrance could tickle your toes.
The daisies just chuckled, their laughter so bright,
As petals would flutter, what a silly sight!

"Oh, dear gentle petal, don't boast so, my friend!"
Said the mischievous violet, her voice on the mend.
"For all of your charm and your shimmery hue,
When the wind starts to blow, we'll all dance too!"

The rose struck a pose, with a wink and a sway,
As the breeze blew so softly, she'd prance and would play.
But the violets, crafty, began to conspire,
To tickle the rose with their soft, flowery choir!

The petals all giggled, as the rose gave a twirl,
She spun round and round, like a dizzying whirl.
So take note of the blooms, and their playful fuss,
In the garden of laughter, there's joy for us!

Reflections in Petal Pools

In a garden so bright and spry,
Reflections dance as bees zoom by.
Petals giggle, they twist and twirl,
While ants hold meetings, not in a whirl.

A daisy claims it's the queen so bold,
While tulips gossip, their petals unfold.
Each flower boasts of its fragrant might,
But bees just buzz, enjoying the sight.

The sun laughs down on this humorous show,
As squirrels practice their acrobatic flow.
With every breeze, the petals delight,
In a world that sparkles, oh what a sight!

So come, take a peek at the joyful spree,
Where flowers chatter and dance full of glee.
The petal pools shimmer in sunlight's beam,
Reflecting dreams in a botanical dream.

Dancing with Dandelion Wishes

Amidst the green, a dance begins,
With dandelions twirling, let's spin, spin, spin!
They're tiny suns with a tuft of hair,
Wishing on whispers that float through the air.

A ladybug joins, in a polka dot style,
While butterflies flutter, wearing a smile.
Each puff is a wish that begins to roam,
While ants form a line, like a parade back home.

So toss a wish into the breeze,
As dandelion seeds swirl with such ease.
Giggles erupt from each tiny stem,
In this playful garden's whimsical gem.

With friends all around, in sun's golden glow,
The dance of the wishes is all for the show.
As the day fades to dusk, with petals so bright,
We'll waltz with the wishes, until the moonlight.

The Haunting of Radiant Blooms

In the moonlight, the flowers sway,
Whispering secrets of the light of day.
A ghostly rose with a petal's sigh,
Claims it knows how to float and fly.

Lilies giggle, hiding their glee,
As the ghost tells tales of a bumblebee.
With a twist and a turn, they start to dance,
Every petal swirling as if in a trance.

The daisies chuckle at the spooky fright,
As shadows play games in the soft moonlight.
"Boo!" says the lily with a bloom so rare,
But the bees keep buzzing, not a single care.

A vibrant haunt where petals take flight,
In a festival held on a starry night.
With laughter and joy, the blooms all declare,
These radiant spirits are beyond compare!

The Forgotten Name of That Flower

There's a flower that whispers, though it's hard to place,
Its name slips my mind, like a forgetful face.
With petals like laughter and humor so sweet,
It tickles the senses, a charming treat.

The bees know it well, they swarm and they buzz,
But I just chuckle, saying, "Oh, what was?"
As butterflies waltz in a flurry of grace,
I can't help but smile at this floral race.

The gardener rolls eyes, "Just look very close!"
But I keep on mixing it up with a ghost.
"Is it Fred?" I ponder, "Or maybe it's Sue?"
I'll just call it happy, it'll have to do!

So when in doubt, I'll just give it a name,
That tickles the tongue and dances with flame.
For flowers may fade, but this fun we'll keep,
With laughter in petals, in memories deep.

Lullabies of the Heart's Garden

In a garden where giggles grow,
Daisies tell tales of a dance with snow.
Sunflowers yawn in a slumberous glow,
While whispers of bees say, "Don't be slow!"

Frogs in the pond play leapfrog and hop,
While sleepy-eyed kittens refuse to stop.
They chase after fireflies, twirl and plop,
In this merry dreamland, laughter won't drop.

Mice wear tiny hats, sip tea on a leaf,
They giggle at shadows, the ultimate thief.
With each little nibble, they spread their belief,
That joy is a treasure beyond any grief.

In this patch of whimsy, we sing and we sway,
As the moon curls up like a cat in the fray.
With lullabies ringing, we'll dance till the day,
For in hearts' gardens, forever we'll play.

The Color of Forgotten Days

Once I lost my marbles in a sea of socks,
And gained a wisdom from laughing at clocks.
Colors of chaos wrapped tight in a box,
While strawberries whisper sweet talks to the rocks.

I painted my hat with a bright sunny hue,
And danced with the shadows of things I once knew.
The sky bursts with giggles, says, "Look, it's true!"
As clouds make a fool of their cottony crew.

Time plays hide-and-seek with a playful grin,
As butterflies marvel at where they've been.
The joy of a splash in a puddle so thin,
Reminds me that laughter is where we begin.

What of those days that waltz by in a blink?
They're clad in the colors of pastel and pink.
With each silent chuckle, I stop just to think,
That memories shimmer, like apple juice, drink.

Traces of an Absent Spring

Oh how the flowers forgot to come out,
A squirrel has taken their route, full of doubt.
He juggles with acorns, then takes a sprout,
While rain clouds above toss a sensitive pout.

The daisies penned letters, begging the sun,
While the tulips just giggled, thinking it fun.
"Let's wear all our colors, we've just begun!"
They planned a parade—oh what a big run!

But where are the breezes with laughter and song?
As chirping frogs croak that the wait's been too long.
"Let's plant our own wishes, and see what goes wrong!"
And thus began spring's wild and whimsical throng.

Now echoes of absence just twirl in the air,
As daisies in dresses perform without care.
With laughter and joy, shaking off every snare,
They hope absent spring comes, but for now, they dare.

Memories Woven with Dew

In a meadow of laughter, the flowers uncoil,
As the sun peeks through with a cheeky smile.
Each dew drop a story, they frolic and toil,
In a world made of giggles, no need for a spoil.

Dance with the daisies, twirl under the sky,
While butterflies tease with their glimmering fly.
Each memory woven, oh my, oh my!
A patchwork of laughter that never says bye.

The tall grass whispers secrets of old,
With every soft breezy touch, it unfolds.
And a frog near the brook croons love songs so bold,
Daring the stars to join in, uncontrolled.

So let's sip the morning, wrapped tight in a hug,
While bees sing their verses, and snuggle the rug.
In this realm of refreshment, so cozy, so snug,
We find all our memories, wrapped warm like a bug.

Ballads of Nature's Quiet Echo

In a grove where squirrels chat,
A bear wears a tiny hat!
The bees buzz a silly tune,
While frogs dance under the moon.

An owl in glasses reads a book,
While rabbits play a game to look.
The trees sway with laughter so bright,
Nature's jokes bring sweet delight.

A raccoon sings with a feathery owl,
The crickets join in with a howl.
Every critter joins in the fun,
In this place, there's room for everyone!

So if you wander under these trees,
Expect laughter on the breeze.
For Nature's tales, they never cease,
In echoing ballads that bring you peace.

The Enchanted Grove of Memories

In an enchanted grove where odd things grow,
The flowers gossip, putting on a show.
The butterflies wear the finest of shoes,
While the mushrooms sip on morning dew blues.

A dancing deer twirls at a frog's soft song,
While the hedgehogs cheer, all sing along.
The sun peeks in, it's a sight to see,
As the breeze tickles the branches, so carefree.

There's laughter woven in satin vines,
And secrets shared through whispered signs.
The bumblebees chuckle, buzzing away,
In this magical grove, come laugh and play!

So gather your friends, let's make a toast,
To the memories made, we cherish the most!
In this enchanted place, joy is key,
Where every heartbeat dances wild and free.

Fables from the Whispering Woods

In the woods where the trees like to gossip loud,
The shadows giggle, all merry and proud.
A snail in socks takes his grandest stroll,
While a cat naps deep in a floral bowl.

The mice hold meetings in moonlit glows,
While the fireflies twinkle like bright little shows.
Each rustle and chatter spins tales anew,
Of a wolf who loved wearing shoes that were blue.

Old badgers trade stories of times from the past,
While the toads throw a potluck, more fun than a blast!
The owls hoot puns that soar through the air,
With chuckles and cackles, a whimsical flair.

So tread lightly on paths where fables unfold,
You'll find laughter and joy more precious than gold.
In the whispering woods, let curiosity bloom,
For every step shared, brings laughter and room!

Storytellers of the Flowering Past

Under blossoms of pink and white so fair,
A rabbit juggles with extraordinary flair.
While snails share tales from their slow and sweet song,
The wind carries chuckles all day long.

The daisies giggle, their petals shake,
As frogs tell stories of the leaps they take.
Ants march in step with a rhythmic beat,
Their dance tells legends, oh so sweet!

There's a parrot who squawks jokes from the trees,
Making everyone laugh with the greatest of ease.
A wise old tortoise recounts tales galore,
Spinning fables of friends who once soared.

So sit on the grass, let the joy unfold,
In every petal, find stories of old.
For these storytellers of the flowering past,
Will fill your heart with laughter that lasts!

Legends Beneath the Moonlight

The owl wears a monocle, quite posh,
He squawks out tales, while the stars all nosh.
The raccoons dance, with hats on their heads,
While night-time gossip fills up their threads.

A squirrel dressed fancy, in velvet and lace,
Claims he's the prince of this wild, green space.
He twirls with his acorns, as if they could sing,
While frogs croak duets to the frogs on the swing.

Beneath the bright moon, odd myths come alive,
Where legends are born, and the forest can thrive.
Each creature with stories, both silly and grand,
In a world full of laughter, they take a stand.

So join in the night, let your worries take flight,
For beneath this moonlight, all things feel right.
With chuckles and glee, let the tales all unfold,
In a forest of fables, both funny and bold.

A Melody of Soft Petals

Daisies do pirouettes, with flowers a-twirl,
While tulips gossip, and violets whirl.
A bumblebee sings, in a buzzing delight,
As petals compose, a sweet song for the night.

The roses wear crowns, made of candy and fluff,
Claiming they're all the best, oh isn't that tough?
A daffodil chimes in, 'I'm yellow and bright!'
As laughter erupts in a flowery fight.

Lifting up voices, the garden's alive,
With echoes of chuckles—come on, let's thrive!
Each bud has a tale, tucked under its leaf,
In a world full of petals, there's joy, not grief.

So sway to the cadence of nature's sweet choir,
Where funny meets fables, and never grows dire.
In this bright palette, where laughter entwines,
May melodies linger, and humor defines.

Silhouettes of Sweet Reminders

In the shadows they dance, those whimsical sprites,
With winks and with giggles, they create funny sights.
A jester of shadows juggles the stars,
While mischievous whispers float near and far.

They slip through the cracks in the walls of your dreams,
Playing pranks on your thoughts, or so it seems.
A riddle of giggles wraps round like a hug,
As they tickle your mind, each thought gives a shrug.

The silhouettes playtag, in a surge of delight,
While the moon gives a chuckle, shining so bright.
Each reminder a jest, not to take life too hard,
For laughter's a treasure, never to discard.

So cherish the flashes of funny disguise,
In the dance of your mind, let laughter arise.
With shadows and whispers, may joy rule the day,
In the realm of sweet fables, where chuckles hold sway.

Murmurs of the Past

The whispers of gardens, where old gnomes once stirred,
Tell tales of their mischief, quite silly, absurd.
With hats far too big, and feet made of stone,
They giggle at memories—their laughter is known.

A cat with a monocle recites all the lore,
Of mice who wore capes, that peeked through the door.
He nods with a grin, while the stories unwind,
Of antics and gaffes, banned from mankind.

The murals of humor on each crumbling wall,
Stand witness to follies, both short and tall.
Each whispering blossom, and rustling inhale,
Breathe life into legends, with fun at the trail.

So listen intently, let laughter be cast,
In the echoes of stories, the murmurs of the past.
For each giggle and chuckle is a memory clear,
In this whimsical tapestry that brings us good cheer.

Fables in the Mist

In a garden so green and bright,
The flowers plotted a tiny flight.
With petals as maps and stems as sails,
They laughed at the tales of their epic trails.

A bumblebee played the role of king,
On wings of laughter, he did wing.
He forgot where he left his golden prize,
But the giggles echoed 'neath the sunny skies.

The daisies danced in a silly line,
With tulips smirking, feeling divine.
"Why was the bee lost?" giggled a rose,
"He should wear glasses, perhaps, I suppose!"

So the flowers formed a parade so grand,
With laughter and giggles, all hand in hand.
In the mist of the morning, with humor so bright,
They spun fables of joy, a whimsical sight.

Petals of an Unseen Dawn

In the twilight, flowers sang a tune,
Of secrets kept under the light of the moon.
They whispered softly, a wild jest,
Of a snail who believed it could fly like the rest.

"Just take a leap from the highest leaf!"
Cackled a petal, in disbelief.
But the snail stood firm, with a grin so wide,
"Patience is key," it said with pride.

With a tumble and roll, it glided down,
Where the daisies laughed and forgot to frown.
In petal conversations filled with cheer,
The snail became a legend, oh, what a year!

So under the unseen light of dawn,
They cherished tales, of fortune and brawn.
With laughter and petals embracing the air,
In this garden of secrets, they flourished with flair.

Glimmers of Loss and Hope

In the glimmers of morning, they'd gather around,
With jokes about squirrels who'd lost their sound.
They'd tell of a bird who forgot its own song,
And the chuckles echoed, all evening long.

A wise old oak watched with a grin,
As the flowers debated where laughter begins.
"Perhaps it's the wind that carries our fate,
Or the sun who decides when it's time to celebrate!"

And through the blooms, a notion took flight,
That each tiny petal sparkled bright.
"Together," they said, "we'll shine through the pain,
With giggles and snickers, like sweet summer rain."

So they danced in the face of loss and despair,
With every misstep, they flourished with flair.
For hope spun in laughter, like threads of a tale,
And they bloomed even brighter when all seemed to pale.

The Chronicle of the Tiny Blossoms

In a cozy nook of the garden's embrace,
Tiny blossoms gathered in a merry place.
"We'll write a chronicle of our shared fun,
Of mishaps and giggles under the sun!"

A dandelion stood up with tales to weave,
"Let's share insights from the wind, I believe!
For every blown seed, there's a story to tell,
Of wispy adventures and where they fell."

And a daffodil chimed in, with humor to boot,
"Remember the time we mistook a root?"
They tumbled in laughter, forgetting their woe,
As they penned their fables, letting joy flow.

With petals of color and spirits so light,
They filled the chronicle deep into the night.
For every tiny blossom carries a view,
Of life's funny fables, timeless and true.

Tales from the Meadow of Lost Dreams

In a meadow so bright, the dreams take a flight,
Chasing butterflies with all of their might.
They trip on a flower, oh what a sight,
Landing in laughter, what a delight!

A cow told a joke, the pigs rolled in glee,
The sheep were quite lost, under a tree.
With a wink and a nod, they sipped their sweet tea,
While the rooster declared, 'Life's silly, just be!'

A rabbit with shades danced under the sun,
Mocking the clouds, saying, 'You can't catch my fun!'
The grass swayed along, everyone was stunned,
For nothing's quite serious when frolicking's begun!

Thus tales in the meadow weave laughter and cheer,
Every bloom tells a joke, every bee brings a tear.
So come take a stroll, let go of your fear,
For the wild dreams of yawns are waiting right here!

The Weight of Each Blue Blossom

A blue blossom sighed, 'I'm heavy today,'
'With tales of the wind that swept me away.'
A snail next to her chuckled, 'You're perfect, hooray!'
'Come dance with the clouds, let your worries decay!'

A squirrel with nuts yelled, 'Why worry so much?'
'Life's lighter than feathers, just add a big touch!'
With a shimmy and gleam, each petal did clutch,
The joy of the day—oh, it tickled them such!

They twirled in the breeze, both near and afar,
The flower and snail, now best friends by a star.
With laughter and giggles, they'd travel bizarre,
Creating new stories, their own memoir!

So next time you see a blue blossom who frowns,
Just offer a smile—remove all the crowns.
For weight's just a laugh, in the land of clowns,
Where colors unite, joy forever abounds!

Roots in the Past

There once was a root with a story to tell,
Of a time when she fell in love with a shell.
She said to a flower, 'Oh, isn't he swell?'
But the flower just giggled, 'You fell? Oh well!'

In the dirt she repented, 'What a blunder I've made!'
The bumblebee buzzed, 'Leave your worries unweighed.'
'Life's deeper than soil, come join the parade,
All roots have their quirks, let the laughter cascade!'

With a twist and a turn, they dug up an old joke,
A worm laughed so hard, he started to choke.
'You call that a root? Just look at my cloak!'
'In my roots, I am rich—let's dance, I'm no bloke!'

Together they sparkled, with joy in the air,
Finding roots in their past, they banished despair.
For laughter, oh laughter, is beyond compare,
In the garden of life, it's the best kind of care!

A Symphony of Fading Colors

A painter once sighed, 'Colors fade in time,'
While hues danced around him, so lost in their rhyme.
With a brush and a giggle, he made a new chime,
Creating a canvas of humor and mime!

There was blue that was snappy, and yellow that spun,
Green laughed aloud, 'Oh, this is such fun!'
'When colors get sad, we just throw them a pun,'
And they twirled and they swayed, as bright as the sun!

But wait! A color felt lonely, all gray,
'Join my party!' the painter cried out in a way.
With cheer and confetti, their blues washed away,
Now the symphony plays, where joy holds sway!

So if your colors wane, just laugh and be bold,
With a wink and a twirl, let the stories unfold.
For fading is nonsense when your heart is pure gold,
In the symphony of life, that never grows old!

www.ingramcontent.com/pod-product-compliance
Lightning Source LLC
Chambersburg PA
CBHW051642160426
43209CB00004B/761